LEARN ABOUT
RAINBOWS

by Golriz Golkar

Published by The Child's World®
1980 Lookout Drive • Mankato, MN 56003-1705
800-599-READ • www.childsworld.com

Design Elements: Shutterstock Images
Photographs ©: Shutterstock Images, cover (rainbow), cover
(jar), 1 (rainbow), 1 (jar), 4 (olive oil), 12, 15; Danny Smythe/
Shutterstock Images, 4 (honey); Elizabeth A. Cummings/
Shutterstock Images, 4 (food coloring), 7, 23; Rick Orndorf,
5; Dale Kelly/Shutterstock Images, 9; Alexander Kalina/
Shutterstock Images, 11; Dorin Ionescu/iStockphoto, 17;
iStockphoto, 19; Francisco Blanco/Shutterstock Images, 20

ISBN 9781503832121
LCCN 2018962805

Printed in the United States of America
PA02420

About the Author

Golriz Golkar is a teacher and
children's author who lives
in Nice, France. She enjoys
cooking, traveling, and looking
for ladybugs on nature walks.

TABLE OF CONTENTS

CHAPTER 1

Let's Make a Rainbow!

Materials
- ☐ Glass jar with lid
- ☐ ¹/₂ cup honey
- ☐ Red, blue, and green food coloring
- ☐ ¹/₂ cup blue dish detergent
- ☐ ¹/₂ cup water
- ☐ ¹/₂ cup olive oil
- ☐ ¹/₂ cup rubbing alcohol

It is a good idea to gather your materials before you begin.

Once you are finished, you should
see the colors of a rainbow.

STEPS

1. Add one drop of blue food coloring to
    the honey. Add one drop of red coloring
    as well. Mix to create purple. Pour the
    honey slowly into the jar.

2. Pour the detergent slowly into the jar.

3. Add three drops of green food coloring to the cup of water. Tilt the jar carefully. Pour the water slowly, making it run down the inside wall of the jar. The colors should not mix.

4. Slowly pour the olive oil on the inside wall of the jar again. This will make yellow.

5. Add three drops of red food coloring to the rubbing alcohol. Mix well. Slowly pour it on the inside wall of the jar. Keep the jar tilted.

Be careful when using food coloring.
It can stain your hands.

6. Place your jar near sunlight. You will see shades of orange and indigo. Then you will have seven colors. Your rainbow is complete!

CHAPTER 2

What Is a Rainbow?

A rainbow looks like a multicolored **arc** in the sky. Its colors are red, orange, yellow, green, blue, indigo, and violet. They always appear in the same order, from outside to inside. The colors in the experiment appear in this order.

DID YOU KNOW?

The name Roy G. Biv can be used to remember the order of colors in a rainbow. Each letter stands for a color.

The seven colors of the rainbow always appear in the same order.

Rainbows are **optical illusions**. They are not solid objects. They do not touch the ground.

CHAPTER 3

How Do Rainbows Form?

Humans see sunlight as white light. White light is really made of different colors. **Rays** from the Sun travel to Earth at different speeds. Rays of different colors travel from the Sun to Earth at different speeds. Purple rays are the fastest. Red rays are the slowest. White light is made when the different colors of light mix.

Sunlight looks white, but it is actually made up of different colors.

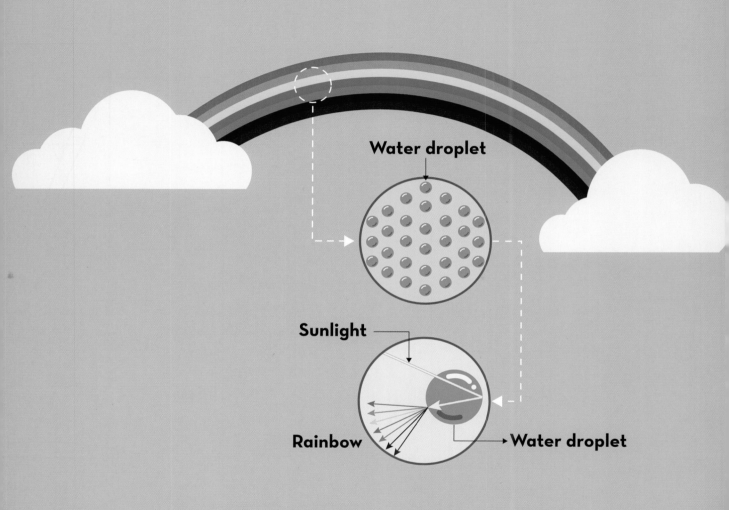

Water droplet

Sunlight

Rainbow

Water droplet

Sunlight reflects and then refracts in
water droplets to form rainbows.

Rainbows form when white light separates back into different colors. The Sun's rays strike water droplets in the **atmosphere**. These droplets might be rain, fog, mist, or dew. The rays **reflect** as they pass through the droplets. The rays are doubled and create a mirror image. The rays also slow down when they enter the droplets. The change in speed causes the rays to **refract**, or bend.

Each ray passes through the droplets at a slightly different angle because of this bend. This forms a color **spectrum** known as a rainbow. It always appears in the direction opposite the Sun. If the Sun is in the east, the rainbow appears to the west.

A rainbow can also be created using a **prism**. The glass bends the light rays at slightly different angles. A rainbow appears.

Objects known as prisms can create
rainbows without water droplets.

CHAPTER 4

What Kinds of Rainbows Are There?

There are several kinds of rainbows. The most common rainbow is the primary rainbow. It forms when light rays are reflected once inside the droplets. Because water droplets are round, rainbows are actually full circles. They only look like arcs from the ground.

Rainbows are really circles.

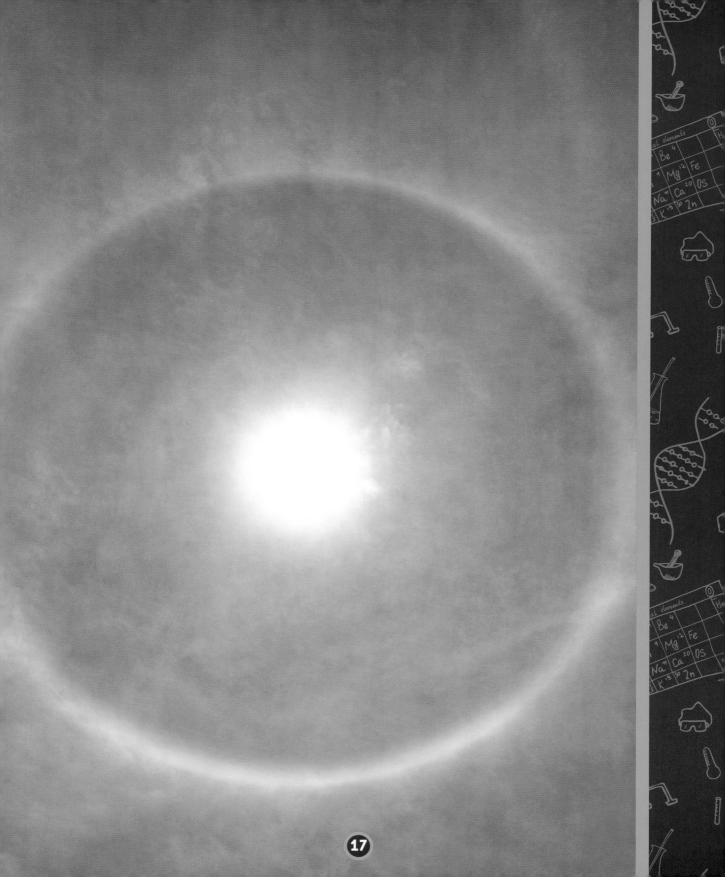

DID YOU KNOW?

Full-circle rainbows may be seen from airplanes.

Light rays might reflect twice. This creates double rainbows. Tertiary (TER-shee-ayr-ee) rainbows have three arcs. Their light is reflected three times. They are very rare. They have weak colors.

Supernumerary (SOO-per-NOO-muh-rayr-ee) rainbows have faintly colored rings. These rings appear inside a primary rainbow.

Supernumerary rainbows are sometimes called stacked rainbows because of their rings.

These rainbows form when light passes through water droplets that are similar in size.

Fogbows do not have the same bright
colors as primary rainbows.

Fogbows are similar to primary rainbows. They form in fog. Their colors are often hard to see.

Moonbows are created by the Moon's reflection of light. They are much dimmer than primary rainbows.

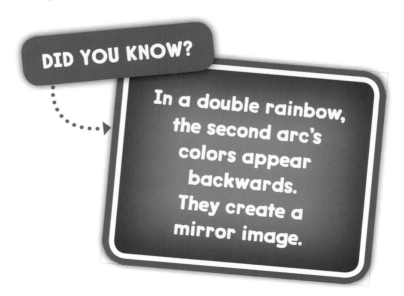

DID YOU KNOW?

In a double rainbow, the second arc's colors appear backwards. They create a mirror image.

Glossary

arc (ARK) An arc is a semi-circle or curved line. Rainbows appear in the shape of an arc.

atmosphere (AT-mos-feer) The atmosphere is made of the gases surrounding the Earth and is often called air. Water droplets in the atmosphere play a role in rainbow formation.

optical illusion (OP-ti-kuhl ih-LOO-zhuhn) An optical illusion is an image that is not what it appears to be. A rainbow is not a physical object; it is an optical illusion in the sky.

prism (PRIZ-uhm) A prism is a clear, solid object, often with a triangular base, that light can pass through. A prism bends light rays to create a rainbow spectrum.

ray (RAY) A ray is a line of light that comes from a light source. Sunlight travels to Earth as rays.

reflect (ri-FLEKT) When something is reflected, a mirror image is created. Light rays reflected twice within water droplets create double rainbows.

refract (ri-FRAKT) Rays like light, sound, and heat refract, or bend, by passing them from one medium into another. A prism refracts the rays of sunlight.

spectrum (SPEK-trum) A spectrum is a band of colors that is formed when light is passed through a prism. The colors of the rainbow represent a spectrum.

To Learn More

In the Library

Bauer, Marion Dane. *Rainbow*. New York, NY: Simon Spotlight, 2016.

McKenzie, Precious. *Rainbows*. Vero Beach, FL: Rourke Educational Media, 2018.

Slingerland, Janet. *What Causes a Rainbow?* Mankato, MN: The Child's World, 2017.

On the Web

Visit our website for links about rainbows: **childsworld.com/links**

Note to Parents, Teachers, and Librarians: We routinely verify our Web links to make sure they are safe and active sites. So encourage your readers to check them out!

Index